MARTIAL ARTS

A TRUE BOOK

by
Bob Knotts

Children's Press®
A Division of Grolier Publishing

New York London Hong Kong Sydney
Danbury, Connecticut

A karate competition

Reading Consultant
Linda Cornwell
*Coordinator of School Quality
and Professional Improvement
Indiana State Teachers
Association*

Author's Dedication:
*With love and appreciation to
Jill and my parents—
thanks for the lessons.*

*The photo on the cover shows
a seven-year-old Japanese girl
doing karate. The photo on the
title page shows a karate class.*

**Visit Children's Press® on the
Internet at:
http://publishing.grolier.com**

Library of Congress Cataloging-in-Publication Data

Knotts, Bob.
    Martial arts / by Bob Knotts.
        p.   cm. — (True book)
    Includes bibliographical references and index.
    Summary: Introduces judo, karate, and several other martial arts,
highlighting safety and the mental discipline involved.
    ISBN 0-516-21609-0 (lib. bdg.)   0-516-27028-1 (pbk.)
    1. Martial arts Juvenile literature. [1. Martial arts.] I. Title.
II. Series.
GV1101.K66 2000
796.8—dc21
                                                                99-15091
                                                                CIP
                                                                AC

GROLIER
PUBLISHING

Contents

A taekwondo competition

What Are Martial Arts?

Martial arts are many things. They are sports. They are ways to protect yourself if someone attacks you. And they are ways to improve your body and your mind.

You may have seen actors use martial arts in the movies. Often, these actors kick and

Many people are familiar with martial arts from seeing action movies.

punch people. They pretend to be tough and mean. They use martial arts to hurt people and to get anything they want. But this is not really what martial arts are all about.

In real life, martial arts require the ability to control oneself. They also require a strong body and a smart mind. Good martial artists avoid fights whenever possible. This is true even when someone

Martial arts build strong bodies and strong minds.

says nasty things to them. Instead of fighting, they walk away so that no one is hurt.

The martial arts were invented thousands of years ago, but no one knows for sure when they began. Buddhist monks may have started martial arts in India more than 2,400 years ago. Monks are priests in the Buddhist religion. The monks needed a way to defend themselves against people who wanted to hurt them. So they

A Chinese
Buddhist monk
practicing
martial arts

learned to use their own
hands and feet and other
body parts for protection.

Martial arts spread to other
countries in Asia, including
China, Korea, and Japan.
Hundreds of different martial

Sculpture of a Japanese samurai (left) and a painting showing a Japanese ninja (right)

arts were invented. Japanese samurai, or warriors, learned some martial arts during their training. So did Japanese ninjas.

Ninjas were secret fighters who wore black uniforms that covered their heads and faces. They became experts in hand-to-hand fighting and in using strange weapons. Some weapons were thrown and some were used to strike enemies. Ninja groups were banned by Japan in the 1600s.

One of today's most popular martial arts, judo, started in Japan. Judo was invented by Dr. Jigoro Kano in the 1880s. Dr. Kano wanted judo to be a

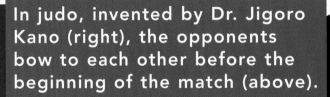

In judo, invented by Dr. Jigoro Kano (right), the opponents bow to each other before the beginning of the match (above).

safer way to practice martial arts. Judo means "the gentle way." It was the first martial art included as a sport in the Olympic Games.

Judo

Judo matches are short and often exciting. Two judokas, or competitors, stand barefoot on a large mat. The mat is called a tatami. The judokas hold onto each other's uniforms when the match starts. The short, loose uniform is called a judogi. Then each competitor

An Olympic women's judo match (left); Judokas hold onto each other's uniforms when the match starts (below).

A judo throw

tries to throw his or her opponent down on the mat quickly.
   A judo throw is a special
way of flipping or tripping an
opponent. Judo has many
types of throws. To do them, a

A shoulder throw

judoka must get an opponent
off balance—leaning in some
direction. A good throw drops
an opponent to the tatami as
fast as you can blink your eye.

In one type of throw, called a
shoulder throw, the judoka
quickly turns and grabs the

opponent under one arm. Then the judoka flips the opponent over a shoulder and onto the tatami.

A good throw scores one point, and the judo match is over. But there are other ways to score a point in this sport. Sometimes both competitors drop to the mat together. When this happens, judo looks a little like wrestling. A judoka then tries to grab the opponent and hold him or her very

Judokas down on the tatami (top);
A good judo hold wins the match (bottom).

tightly. There are many ways to do this in judo. These are called holds. A good judo hold will also win the match.

In judo, men and women compete separately. Each contestant competes against someone of about the same weight as themelves. This is because heavier people are often stronger.

There are many important competitions for judokas, including the Jigoro Kano Cup

An Olympic men's judo match

and the Pan-American Games. But the most important competition in judo takes place during the Summer Olympics. Judo became an Olympic sport in 1964. Women's judo was added to the Olympic Games in 1992.

Antonius Geesink

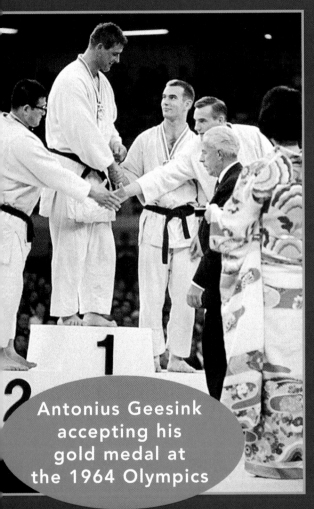

Antonius Geesink accepting his gold medal at the 1964 Olympics

Japanese experts once believed that size didn't matter in judo—that skill was more important. They thought a skilled Japanese judoka could defeat a much bigger opponent. But they changed their minds when Antonius Geesink won the world championship in 1961.

Geesink, who was from The Netherlands, was a great judoka—and a big man. He beat three excellent Japanese fighters in a row. He was the first world champion who wasn't Japanese. In 1964, Geesink won the Olympic gold medal—the first-place award.

Karate

Karate, another martial art, is very different from judo. Karate is a Japanese word that means "empty hand." Karate got this name because karate experts use no weapons except their own body. They may punch an opponent with a fist or the side of one hand, or

Karate training at
a park in Canada

they may strike an opponent
with their fingers, elbows, or
wrists.

Young karate students (top) and a karate kick (bottom)

Karate also uses many kicks. It is important that karate students learn the correct way to do all the punches and kicks. It is also important for students to become both quick and strong as they practice. Often, people shout when they do a karate kick or punch. This helps give them extra strength for an instant.

Many types of karate are taught in martial-arts schools. Each is different from the

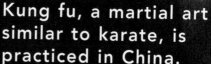

others in some ways. One type of karate began in China. Another type started in Japan.

Taekwondo, one of the most popular types of karate, came from Korea. Taekwondo was

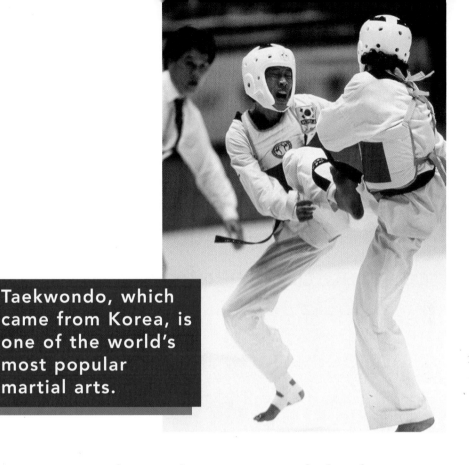

Taekwondo, which came from Korea, is one of the world's most popular martial arts.

introduced as a medaled Olympic sport at the 2000 Olympic Games in Sydney, Australia. Men and women compete separately, just as they do in judo.

Taekwondo means "the way of hands and feet." Competitors wear a dobok—a uniform that looks a lot like a judogi. Also, competitors wear no shoes in a taekwondo match.

In taekwondo, kicks are very important. For example, a competitor may kick an opponent with the side of one foot. Some kicks are made with the heel or even with the ball of the foot.

Athletes wear lots of padding to protect themselves from injury. And, of course, they must

Kicks are very important in taekwondo.

fight by the rules. Only certain kicks and punches are allowed during a taekwondo match.

In competition, no one tries to hurt anyone else. The competitors try only to score points with solid kicks and punches.

Sometimes competitors use
more than one kick or punch at
the same time. The opponent
tries to block these blows and
then strike back. The competitor with the most points at the
end wins.

Safety First

Karate students wearing safety equipment

The most important thing to understand about martial arts is: don't try them without first getting lessons from an expert! Also, never use martial arts to hurt anyone unless they are trying to hurt you! Remember that athletes in karate matches wear lots of safety equipment. It is very easy to hurt someone if you practice martial arts on them!

A teacher demonstrating judo to his students

Other Martial Arts

Judo and karate are two of the most popular martial arts, but there are many others. Jujitsu is an old Japanese martial art that teaches people how to defend themselves against attackers. Jujitsu students learn throws and holds like those used in judo. They also learn

Jujitsu

kicks and punches like those
used in karate. They learn many
other things, too, including how
to use some unusual weapons.

In aikido, one learns how to turn back an opponent's attacks without attacking back.

Aikido is another type of martial art that is good for self-defense. Aikido uses different holds to stop attacks. Students also learn how to twist an attacker's wrist so that the attacker can't hurt anyone.

An unusual Japanese martial art is kendo. In kendo, students learn to sword fight with long bamboo sticks. Opponents face each other and swing their bamboo swords. Teachers show students many ways to

strike an opponent with the sword. They also show how a sword can block hits from an opponent.

Black Belts

The color of a karate student's belt tells how experienced the student is.

The colored belt worn with a uniform is important in judo, karate, and many other martial arts. Lighter-colored belts show that someone is a newer student. Darker belts show that the person has practiced a long time. A black belt is the goal for many martial-arts students. A black belt proves someone is an expert.

For the Body and Mind

Many people learn martial arts as a type of physical exercise. They use judo, karate, or other martial arts to improve their bodies. Students must learn special ways of moving their arms, legs, hips, and shoulders. Then they must practice these movements

over and over. Martial arts help make the body stronger and healthier.

Martial arts are excellent forms of exercise.

But martial arts can also be very good for a person's mind. Students learn to have a positive attitude—to

Martial arts improve the mind as well as the body.

believe they can do whatever they really try to do. They also learn to control strong feelings in different situations. For

A karate
demonstration

example, martial-arts students
learn not to panic if they are
attacked. People who panic
often do the wrong things out

of fear. So students practice staying calm during an attack in order to use their martial arts skills.

Remember that the best martial artists are not like the tough actors in the movies. They try to avoid trouble. They know martial arts are not meant for beating people up. Experts use martial arts to build strong bodies and minds. For them, martial arts are a way of life.

To Find Out More

Here are some additional resources to help you learn more about martial arts:

 **Books**

Metil, Luana, and Townsend, Jace. **The Story of Karate.** Lerner Publications, 1995.

Queen, J. Allen. **Complete Karate.** Sterling Publishing. 1993.

Rafkin, Louise. **The Tiger's Eye, The Bird's Fist.** Little, Brown & Co., 1997.

Sandelson, Robert. **Combat Sports.** Crestwood House, 1991.

Wallechinsky, David. **The Complete Book of the Summer Olympics.** Little, Brown & Co., 1996.

Organizations and Online Sites

Black Belt for Kids
http://www.blackbeltmag.com/bbkids/

Martial-arts information, news, resources, a dictionary of terms, games and puzzles, personalities, and much more.

International Judo Federation (IJF)
http://www.ijf.org

This page can tell you about the organization that supervises all international judo events.

International Olympic Committee (IOC)
http://www.olympic.org

Find out about the organization that runs all Olympic Games.

United States Olympic Committee (USOC)
Olympic House
One Olympic Plaza
Colorado Springs, CO
80909-5760
http://www.usoc.org

The United States Olympic Committee supervises Olympic activity for the United States. Its website includes everything you might want to know about Olympic sports, past and present.

U.S. Taekwondo Union
One Olympic Plaza
Colorado Springs, CO
80909

The U.S. Taekwondo Union supervises taekwondo events for United States athletes.

Important Words

dobok uniform worn in taekwondo

judo martial art that uses throws and holds to defeat an opponent; focuses on overcoming an opponent by skill rather than sheer strength

judogi uniform worn in judo

karate martial art in which all parts of the body are used to punch, strike, kick, or block an opponent

ninjas Japanese secret fighters who were experts in martial arts

samurai Japanese warriors who were skilled in a wide variety of martial arts

taekwondo martial art invented in Korea; it is considered the most popular martial art in the world

tatami mat where a judo match takes place

Index

Meet the Author

Bob Knotts is the author of five True Books on Summer Olympic sports. He also writes for national magazines, including *Sports Illustrated*, *Reader's Digest*, *Family Circle*, *Travel & Leisure*, and *USA Weekend*. He has worked as a newspaper reporter as well as in radio and television. He has been nominated twice for the Pulitzer Prize. Mr. Knotts resides with his wife, Jill, at their home near Fort Lauderdale, Florida.